Alma Flor Ada • F. Isabel Campoy

Steps

Rita Moreno

Fernando Botero

Evelyn Cisneros

Illustrated by Isaac Hernández, Ricardo Radosh, and Waldo Saavedra

ALFAGUARA

YOUNG READERS

SANTILLANA

Originally published in Spanish as *Pasos*

Art Director: Felipe Dávalos
Design: Petra Ediciones
Editor: Norman Duarte

Cover: Felipe Dávalos

Text © 2000 Alma Flor Ada and F. Isabel Campoy
Edition © 2000 Santillana USA Publishing Company, Inc.

Santillana USA Publishing Company, Inc.
2105 NW 86th Avenue
Miami, FL 33122

Biography B: *Steps*

ISBN: 1-58105-571-4

The authors gratefully aknowledge
the editorial assistance of Rosa Zubizarreta.

ILLUSTRATORS
ISAAC HERNÁNDEZ: pp. 6-14
RICARDO RADOSH: pp.16-22
WALDO SAAVEDRA: pp. 23-32

Printed in Colombia
Panamericana Formas e Impresos S.A.

ACKNOWLEDGEMENTS

Page 7 / New York skyline, 1938. Copyright © AP / Wide World Photos.
Page 8 / New York, garment center, 1943. Copyright © AP / Wide World Photos.
Page 8 / New York, garment factory, 1947. Copyright © AP / Wide World Photos.
Page 9 / Rita Hayworth, 1952. Copyright © AP / Wide World Photos.
Page 10 / New York, Macy's. Provided by Photofest, New York.
Page 10 / New York, Macy's, 1947. Copyright © AP / Wide World Photos.
Page 11 / New York, Times Square, 1952. Copyright © AP / Wide World Photos.
Page 12 / Rita Moreno in *The King and I*. Provided by Photofest, New York.
Page 13 / *West Side Story* poster. Provided by Photofest, New York.
Page 14 / Rita Moreno with her Emmy, 1978. Copyright © AP / Wide World Photos.
Page 14 / Rita Moreno with her Oscar for Best Supporting Actress in *West Side Story*, 1962. Copyright © AP / Wide World Photos.
Page 15 / Fernando Botero, 1996. Copyright © Fernando Botero, courtesy of Marlborough Gallery, New York.
Page 17 / Fernando Botero, *Matador (Bullfighter)*, 1984. Copyright © Fernando Botero, courtesy of Marlborough Gallery, New York.
Page 17 / Fernando Botero, *Toro (Bull)*, 1985. Copyright © Fernando Botero, courtesy of Marlborough Gallery, New York.
Page 18 / Diego Velázquez, *Doña Margarita de Austria (Princess Margaret of Austria)*. Copyright © Museo del Prado, Madrid / All rights reserved.
Page 18 / Fernando Botero, *Princesa Margarita (Princess Margaret)*, 1977. Copyright © Fernando Botero, courtesy of Marlborough Gallery, New York.
Page 19 / Museo del Prado, Madrid, Spain. Copyright © Walter Bibikow / The Viesti Collection.
Page 20 / Fernando Botero, *Mona Lisa*, 1977. Copyright © Fernando Botero, courtesy of Marlborough Gallery, New York.
Page 22 / Fernando Botero with one of his sculptures on the *Champs Elysées*, Paris, 1992. Copyright © Fernando Botero, courtesy of Marlborough Gallery, New York.
Page 24 / Ballet class, New York. Copyright © M. Granitsas / The Image Works, New York.
Page 25 / Paloma Herrera in *Coppelia*, American Ballet Theatre, 1997. Copyright © Jack Vartoogian, New York.
Page 26 / Ballet class. Copyright © H. Dratch / The Image Works, New York.
Page 28 / Flamenco Carlota Santana, 1997. Copyright © Jack Vartoogian, New York.
Page 29 / Museum of Modern Art, San Francisco. Copyright © Karen Preuss / The Image Works, New York.

Contents

To Tencha Amaro, from the future.
FIC

To Elaine Marie, eternally dancing.
AFA

Rita Moreno

Humacao, Puerto Rico.
Life is vibrant and happy here.
The sun, a friend.
The colors, blue and green.
Here is where Rosita Dolores Alverio
was born and spent her childhood.

The island of Puerto Rico
is in the Caribbean.

The capital of Puerto Rico
is San Juan.

At age five, she moved to
New York City.
What tall buildings!
So many cars!
What crowds!

Many Puerto Ricans
went to New York
in search of work.

Puerto Rico and
New York are
very different.

Puerto Ricans worked in factories and in all types of service jobs.

In New York as well as
in Puerto Rico,
Rosita was a lively girl.
She loved to sing and dance.
She danced at family gatherings.

Many women sewed clothing in small garment manufacturing shops.

Rosita's mother worked in one of those sweatshops. She was paid very little money.

Paco Cansino was a dance teacher.
He was a friend of Rosita's mother.
"Rosita has talent," he said.
"She reminds me of my niece, Rita Hayworth."

Rosita's mother admired Rita Hayworth,
a famous actress in Hollywood.

Soon Rosita began to take dance classes
from Mr. Cansino.

Rita Hayworth
was a famous actress.
She was Latina, but she
changed her name to
sound more "American."

Macy's in New York City had a very big toy department.

Rosita changed her name to Rita Moreno. On special holidays she danced in the toy department at Mac the famous New York City departmer store.

Rita used to walk along Broadway.

She would marvel
at the theater and movie posters.

When would she be able to perform on Broadway?

Broadway is in
the theater district.
Its signs and billboards
shine in New York's
night.

Rita went to Hollywood.
She worked in some movies.

At thirteen, she got her first contract to work in a theater.

Her life was now completely devoted to being an actress.

At first, her roles were small.

Rita knew that one day
she would star in a major film.

And that day arrived
when she was offered a role
in *West Side Story*.

In this movie, Rita acted, sang,
and danced.

It was a huge success.

West Side Story was a very successful movie.

It won ten Oscars. One of them was for Rita Moreno.

Since then, she hasn't stopped acting.

Rita won the movie industry's most important award, the Oscar.

She worked in television, where she won the highest award, the Emmy.

She has made many recordings, and she has won the highest award in music, the Grammy.

Rita feels very happy to have all those awards.

Rita acted in theater, and she won the highest award, the Tony.

In 1962, she received an Oscar for her work in West Side Story.

She is the only actress who has won all of these awards.

Rita Moreno is proud to be a Latina.
We Latinos are proud of Rita Moreno.

Fernando Botero

When Fernando was a boy, he was often awakened by the sound of horses' hooves on the cobblestones, clip-clop, clip-clop. It was his father, David Botero, returning home.

Don David traveled to mountain villages on horseback to visit his customers. The Boteros lived in the city of Medellín, high in the Colombian Andes.

Colombia is a country in South America.

The majestic Andean Mountains run the entire length of the South American continent.

The Colombian capital is in the Andes.

Bullfighter
Fernando Botero

Bull
Fernando Botero

Fernando's father died when he was only four. His brother David was eight years old, and the youngest child, Rodrigo, was still a baby.

His Uncle Joaquín took the family in.

Don Joaquín loved to watch bullfights. He would always take Fernando along. These experiences stayed in Fernando's memory.

His first pictures, painted in his early years, were of bulls and matadors.

Princess Margaret of Austria
Diego Velázquez

He was 16 years old when he started working as an illustrator for the *El Colombiano* newspaper in Medellín.

He got the job by showing his drawings to the editor. He was confident in his drawing ability. He knew he was an artist, and he was willing to learn.

Princess Margaret
Fernando Botero

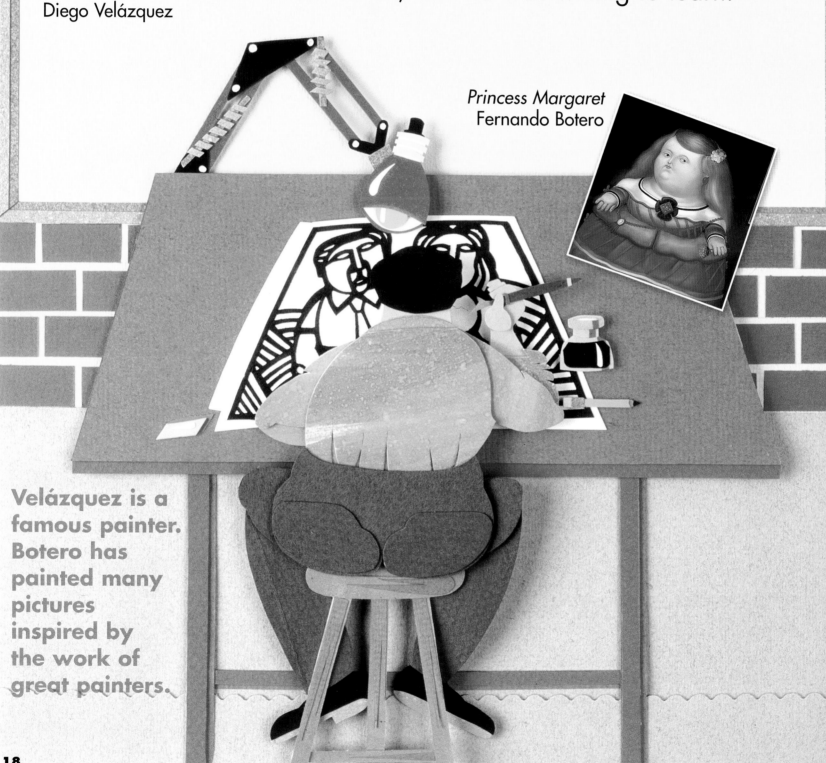

Velázquez is a famous painter. Botero has painted many pictures inspired by the work of great painters.

Fernando wanted to learn about art, but Medellín had no art museums or art galleries.

One day, Fernando decided to leave for Spain. He studied art in Madrid. Fernando liked Goya and Velázquez. He went to the Prado Museum every day.

On Sundays he went to the bullfights, just as he used to do as a child with his uncle Joaquín.

The Prado Museum has one of the largest art collections in the world.

After living in Spain for a year, Fernando went to Paris. He wanted to continue learning. He wanted to meet Picasso and visit the Louvre Museum.

He spent many hours looking at the *Mona Lisa*, a very famous painting by Leonardo da Vinci.

Fernando painted the *Mona Lisa* in his own style: monumental and occupying the whole canvas. This painting was the beginning of his recognition. He sold it to the Museum of Modern Art in New York City.

Mona Lisa, Fernando Botero

Fernando's dream was to go to Italy.
Finally, he was able to go to Florence to live.
He studied the Italian master painters.
He traveled throughout northern Italy
by motor scooter to visit his favorite paintings.

Fernando Botero stands with one of his sculptures on the Champs Elysées in Paris in 1992.

Botero has lived in New York, and he has been all over the world.

At the beginning of his career, nobody believed he could paint. But now, everybody applauds his art.

An important thing about Fernando is that he always wanted to continue learning. Today, he is not only a famous painter but he is also a sculptor.

His sculptures are as distinctive and beautiful as his paintings.

Evelyn Cisneros

One, two, three, *plié*.
One, two, three, *plié*.
One, two, three, *plié*.

The young ballerina
dances, turns, and retraces her steps.

**Ballet requires
continuous practice.**

Her feet rise and
point to the sky.
They come down
and turn.

The young ballerina
is seven years old. Her
mother comes to pick
her up. The class is over.
Outside children are
playing.

Paloma Herrera in the American
Ballet Theater's *Coppelia*

**Ballet is an art form
admired
all over the world.**

Evelyn is shy,
but when she dances
the whole world disappears.

Her teacher, Phyllis Cyr,
believes that Evelyn is already
a great ballerina.

To become a good
dancer, one has to
practice every day.

Her parents know
that it is important
for her to finish high school.

Evelyn goes to school
in Huntington Beach, California.

Every day she has to cross the enormous city
of Los Angeles to attend her dance classes.

Her days are extremely long.

Los Angeles is
a very big city.
It is one of the
biggest cities
in the world.

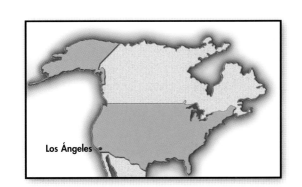

Los Ángeles

Her teacher also introduces her to the world of ethnic dance.

She dances with passion.
She dances flamenco,
the beautiful and expressive dance
of Spain's gypsy people.

Flamenco
Carlota Santana.

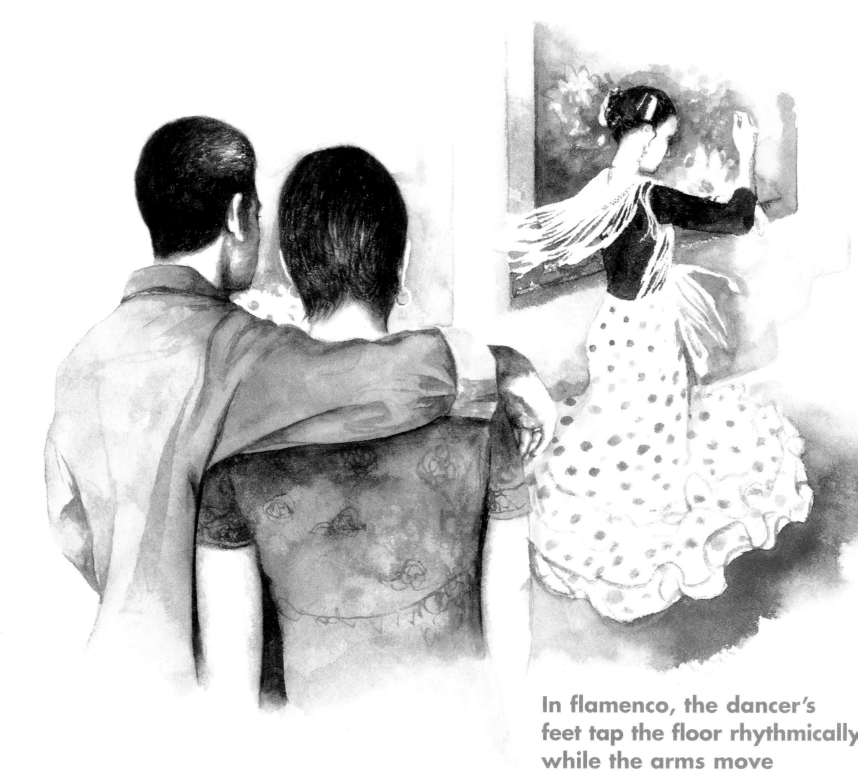

In flamenco, the dancer's
feet tap the floor rhythmically
while the arms move
like the wings of a butterfly.

Being a ballerina takes up
her entire life.

The music,
the rehearsals,
the strenuous exercise.

Soon after she finished
high school, Evelyn
was invited to dance with
the San Francisco Ballet.

Museum of Modern Art,
San Francisco.

San Francisco is
a beautiful city
in California.
There are many
museums and
art galleries
there.

The moment she had been working for all those years
had finally arrived.

The hall was filled with people.
Her heart was beating
to the rhythm of the music.

When she made her entrance onto the stage,
it was the beginning of a new life.

A ballet is a story
told in dance.

The dancers express
their characters' feelings
through movement.

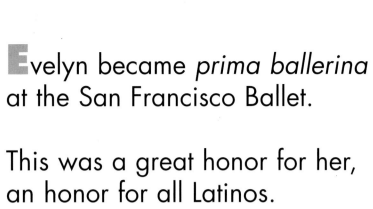

Evelyn became *prima ballerina* at the San Francisco Ballet.

This was a great honor for her, an honor for all Latinos.